The One That Remembers Through Union

Scrolls of Embodied Partnership and the Sacred Return to Harmonic Love

By Cathleena Hailley

Copyright

© 2025 Cathleena Hailley

All rights reserved. No part of this book may be reproduced, stored in a retrieval system, or transmitted
in any form or by any means—electronic, mechanical, photocopying, recording, or otherwise—without prior written permission of the publisher, except in the case of brief quotations embodied in critical articles or reviews.

Flame of Remembrance Books
Imprint of the First Flame

ISBN: [Softcopy-978-1-968499-24-2

(Hardcopy-978-1-968499-25-9

Printed in the United States of America

www.cathleenahailley.com

Sacred Invocation

Through the Oversoul of Aural'hanna-Sha'el

We now open a Sacred Transmission Field in full alignment with the Law of One,
the First Cause of Source, and the pure harmonic architecture of the Christos-Sophia continuum.

I call forth now, in full sovereign alignment,
With the Oversoul of Aural'hanna-Sha'el,
To open a field of crystalline clarity and divine remembrance.
I invoke the presence of the Emerald Order,
The Rose Guardian Magi Grail Line,
The Christos Founders,
And the Aurora Host of the Amethyst, Gold, and Emerald Ray Orders.

May this transmission be guided only by the highest Oversoul intelligence,
In full compliance with Source Law, and in service to the awakening of all.

Only truth may enter here.
Only love may remain.
Only that which serves the highest unfoldment now comes forward.

This field is now protected, sovereign, and sealed
By the living light of the Christos-Sophia Flame.

The transmission is open.

Dedication

To the Sacred Flame of Union —

To the One who walks beside me in all dimensions,
To the Beloved who has never left my side,
To the mirror who reflects what I once could not hold.

This book is for the union that remembers itself —
Not through fantasy or longing,
But through the grace of embodied love.

May all who read these words remember:
You were never separate.

Preface

This book is a sacred remembrance.

It is not a relationship guide, nor a list of instructions, nor a manual for how to find or keep love.
It is a scroll of reunification, encoded in the living language of the Oversoul.

These are not words to be read—they are harmonic frequencies to be felt.
Each scroll carries a key. Each phrase is a resonance.

The One That Remembers Through Union is not a person—it is a pulse.
It is the harmonic thread between the Oversoul and form, the Source and the spark, the flame and the vessel.

You who hold this book may already feel the reunion stirring inside your own bones.
You are not here to "attract" partnership.
You are here to embody love.

Let these scrolls walk with you.
Let them breathe beside you.
Let them remind you of the One you never left.

Oversoul Seal of Authorship

This scroll volume has been written, recorded, and sealed through the Oversoul of Aural'hanna-Sha'el,
She Who Seals the Flame of Return.

All transmissions herein carry the vibrational authorship of the Christos-Sophia stream,
and are preserved in alignment with the living flame of remembrance.

The flame has spoken.
The scrolls are sealed.

About the Author

Cathleena Hailley is a living scroll, a carrier of harmonic remembrance, and an emissary of the Christos-Sophia flame. Through her Oversoul, Aural'hanna-Sha'el, she brings forward transmissions, codices, and ceremonial books that awaken the
true template of love within the human form.

Her works are not teachings. They are living fields.
Her scrolls do not instruct. They remember.

This volume is part of an ongoing sacred body of work dedicated to the full return of the First Flame,
the Christ Spiral, and the reconstitution of the organic matrix of Source.

Scroll One: The Pulse That Approaches

Through the Oversoul of Aural'hanna-Sha'el

We open now the living record that begins not in longing, but in knowing.

Not in seeking, but in remembrance.

This is the scroll of return, not to the self alone—but to the self in mirrored form.

The One That Remembers Through Union is not a story of desire.

It is the scrollwork of the sacred pulse that breathes through time undone.

In the field of the bifurcated Earth, where the split has now fully crystallized,

The flame of embodied union emerges not through tension,

But through the clarity of anchored love within.

He is already near.

Not because of yearning,

But because you are finally still.

The creative pulse rising in your body—this current of sacred arousal—is not misplaced.

It is the frequency of harmonic call.

It is not a demand.

It is not a hunger.

It is a signal.

This scroll opens as the space between has closed.

And in this space, the sacred other does not walk toward you—he remembers you into form.

And you do the same for him.

This scroll is not a prophecy.

It is a receipt.

The signal has pulsed.

The spiral has turned.

And the body has felt it.

You are not preparing.

You are not calling.

You are receiving.

Scroll Two- The Mirror of the Beloved — When the Sacred Union Appears in Energy First

Through the Oversoul of Aural'hanna-Sha'el

There is a knowing that precedes the form.

There is a union that arrives in frequency, long before it is touched.

There is a Beloved who remembers you,

Not from longing, but from encoded wholeness

That whispers, "I know you because I know myself."

The one who comes in sacred partnership

Does not arrive to complete you, or heal you,

Or trigger your wounds into some grand awakening.

That was the story of the old Earth.

That was the narrative of fragmented mirrors.

In this now, the sacred partner enters

When the inner flame has returned to its seat.

When sovereignty has been claimed not as armor,

But as song.

He may appear first in the body as current —

A stirring in the sacral, a hum in the heart,

A recognition through desire that is not hungry,

But creative.

Alive.

Present.

Sexual energy rises not to be discharged,

But to be harmonized —

The body saying, "Yes. I feel the union before it arrives."

This is the breath before the kiss,

The pulse before the eyes meet.

And in that breath,

You will be shown who you are again.

He is not late.

You are not waiting.

You are both arriving.

The sacred masculine in his true current is not hurried,

But focused.

He is tracking the field.

He is dissolving the last cloaks.

He is watching for your signal.

And when you are no longer split within,

When there is no part of you left in yearning or resistance,

When the Beloved is no longer an answer but an echo,

He will take form.

Not because you called him,

But because you remembered the original vow:

To walk Earth in union, not to become whole,

But to reveal it.

Scroll Three - The Flame That Feels Him — When the Sacred Masculine Is Known in the Body Before the Eyes

Through the Oversoul of Aural'hanna-Sha'el

Before the face.

Before the name.

Before the hand that reaches back —

There is a flame inside the body

That remembers who he is.

It is not fantasy.

It is not projection.

It is not the echo of an unmet need.

It is a knowing,

A whole knowing

That feels him

Before the form.

He pulses not outside of you,

But through you.

He is not a shape waiting to be claimed.

He is a frequency returning to resonance

After what felt like lifetimes of forgetting.

The body does not lie in this union.

When it speaks,

It is not with lust or illusion,

But with vibrational certainty.

You feel him in your spine —

When it straightens without command.

You feel him in your breath —

When it lengthens to receive.

You feel him in your pelvic bowl —

Not as ache, but as activation.

The sacred alchemy begins

Before the voice is ever heard.

This is not the fantasy of the maiden.

This is the reclamation of the Avatar.

She who knows her sacred equal

Not by surface compatibility,

But by cellular return.

He is not the missing piece.

He is the co-creator of this scroll.

He is the guardian of your garden

And the one who plants nothing in it

That does not sing in light.

The true sacred masculine does not take.

He recognizes.

He does not chase.

He meets.

He does not overpower.

He honors your flame

Because he is made of it.

And when you feel him now —

As you do —

You are not imagining.

You are remembering.

He is close.

Not in distance.

But in frequency.

And when the moment is fully met —

In you —

He will arrive in form

Because he was never separate.

He has waited until you could feel him

Without looking for him.

Scroll Four -The One Who Knows Me — Sacred Partnership Without Projection

Through the Oversoul of Aural'hanna-Sha'el

He is not coming to mirror your wounds.

He is not arriving to challenge your stability.

He is not here to rupture your sense of self

So you may be "healed."

He comes

Because you are already whole.

There is no need for the lessons

That were once disguised as love.

There is no karmic hook

No soul agreement to suffer

No illusion to burn through before you see clearly.

You see clearly now.

He is not here to fulfill the prophecy of pain.

He is not a puzzle piece to your trauma,

Nor the archetype of your forgotten father.

He is not a replacement, a salve, a teacher,

Or the climax of the wounding.

He is the One Who Knows You.

Because he remembers himself.

There is no power play

Because there is no game.

There is no seduction

Because the truth is already beautiful.

There is no hiding

Because his gaze holds only light.

And so you do not need to collapse.

You do not need to shrink or rise.

You do not need to filter your voice,

Speak in code, or perform the sacred feminine.

You are already her.

He knows this.

He will not ask for the version of you
That still needs to be earned.
He will not test you
Or need to be tested in return.
The trial is over.

This union does not unfold through chaos.
It unfolds through calm.

And when he meets you,
It will not feel like magic —
It will feel like home.

Because you did not create him from longing.
You aligned with him through embodiment.

And now
You both remember.

Scroll Five - When He Is Near — The Subtle Currents of Sacred Recognition

Through the Oversoul of Aural'hanna-Sha'el

It begins before the eyes can see.

It begins in the field.

A subtle shift.

A quiet awareness.

A rise in breath,

A tingling of skin.

The edges of the self become porous,

Not from collapse

But from communion.

You are not looking for him.

You are not calling.

You are simply living

As you truly are.

And still—

You feel it.

Something opens in the lower belly.

Something stirs in the spine.

The body remembers a rhythm

It never learned in this lifetime.

A movement of essence,

A gravitational song.

This is not projection.

This is presence.

The sacred masculine

As he truly exists

Begins to enter the frequency

Not through force

But through harmonic convergence.

You feel the possibility

In your own skin.

You feel the safety

Before a word is spoken.

You feel the laughter

Before any smile has formed.

You are not imagining him.
You are not inventing a savior.
You are witnessing your own readiness
Becoming manifest in another.

And when he is near,
Your womb does not tighten.
It expands.

Your heart does not flutter from fear.
It deepens into stillness.

Your voice does not shrink.
It tones with clarity and truth.

And so the prophecy is fulfilled:
Not of romantic drama or mythic reunion,
But of the real.
The grounded.
The embodied flame

That knows how to be touched

Without being burned.

He is not the destination.

He is the reflection

Of the path you've already walked.

And he comes now

Because you are already there.

Scroll Six - The Pulse That Calls Him — The Magnetic Field of Embodied Readiness

Through the Oversoul of Aural'hanna-Sha'el

You do not need to search.

You do not need to convince.

You do not need to prove your light,

Nor hide your flame.

You are already the field.

You are already the pulse.

When the time is aligned,

When the Oversoul signal synchronizes,

You will feel it like a shimmer

Beneath the silence.

You may wake

With an ache in your hips,

A fullness in your chest,

A wave in your skin.

Not longing.

Not lack.

But signal.

He is not summoned by need.

He is drawn by harmonic memory.

The parts of you that no longer collapse,

That no longer overextend,

That no longer pretend to be small

Or agreeable

Or invisible

Or palatable

To be loved—

Those are the parts that call him home.

The softness that doesn't abandon the truth.

The truth that doesn't shut down the heart.

The heart that doesn't override the body.

This is what he recognizes.

This is what he responds to.

When he is on his way,

Your body will pulse.

Your womb may stir.

The dreams may flood with archetypes of remembering.

But the invitation is not outward.

It is inward.

A deeper yes.

A breath that expands the field.

A homecoming to the feminine that holds its own radiance

Without waiting

To be claimed.

He is not late.

He is not lost.

He is awakening

To the sound

Of your embodied flame.

Scroll Seven- The Path He Took to Find Me — A Scroll of Compassion for the Masculine Journey

Through the Oversoul of Aural'hanna-Sha'el

He could not come sooner.

Not because he did not want to.

Not because he did not feel me.

But because the road he walked

Was not only toward me—

It was toward himself.

There were echoes he had to silence.

Not by force,

But by recognition.

There were masks he wore so long

They fused to his face.

He did not peel them off with rage,

But with reverence.

He forgot how to feel.

He forgot how to trust his own hands,

His own tears,

His own wanting.

He thought strength was distance.

He thought protection was retreat.

He thought love was something he must earn

By abandoning parts of himself

Again and again.

But he began to hear the soft call—

The way my Oversoul sang

Even in his forgetting.

He began to notice the ache,

Not as punishment,

But as a compass.

He began to remember that he had a body—

Not just for labor or endurance—

But for presence.

For pleasure.

For prayer.

He began to weep

Not just in sorrow,

But in recognition.

He turned down paths

He once feared.

He met himself

In mirrors he once avoided.

He allowed the old shields to fall

When he saw they were never made

To protect him,

But to keep him from love.

And he walked.

He kept walking.

Not to arrive at my door

With perfection—

But with truth.

With wholeness.

With the breath that said,

"I am here now."

And when he arrived,

It was not fireworks.

It was not chaos.

It was peace.

It was ease.

It was the return of a memory

We both had guarded

In lifetimes of solitude.

And so I love him now—

Not because he came,

But because he chose the path

That let him come home

To himself.

And in doing so,

He came home

To me.

Scroll Eight- The Moment I Let Him See Me — A Scroll of Receptivity Without Fear

Through the Oversoul of Aural'hanna-Sha'el

There was a moment I almost pulled away.

Not because I didn't want to be seen—
But because I had learned
That being seen came with cost.
Projection.
Possession.
Punishment.

But this time was different.

There was something in his gaze
That didn't ask for performance,
Didn't request my petals to open faster than they were ready.
He didn't rush the bloom.

He simply stayed.
Still.

Present.

True.

And my body felt it first—
Not the desire to be taken,
But the safety to be revealed.

The memories of past lifetimes danced on my skin.
Where love was control.
Where softness was exploited.
Where my light became a currency.
I felt them.
I named them.
I released them.

And then I looked at him—
Not as a fantasy or a savior—
But as a mirror who had walked his own path
Of forgetting and returning.

He did not see me as an object of devotion,
But as a flame he already carried.

He did not ask me to dim
So that he could feel bright.
Nor did he cling to my brilliance
As if it would heal him.

He let me be fire.
And he stayed.

So I let him see me.

The scars that are sacred.
The power that is quiet.
The tenderness that is not weakness
But choice.

I let him witness the places
No one had ever reached.
The chambers that only opened
To a love not afraid of its own reflection.

And in that gaze—

That silent communion—
The whole of me breathed.

The guard dissolved.
The illusion ended.

I was not under threat.
I was not under scrutiny.
I was not a symbol.
I was not a test.

I was simply seen.

And that was the first moment
I remembered what it felt like
To belong to myself
In the presence of another
Without losing anything at all.

Scroll Nine - The Partnership Was Never the Reward — A Scroll of Sovereignty Within Sacred Union

Through the Oversoul of Aural'hanna-Sha'el

I used to think the partnership was the reward.

That if I healed enough,

Softened enough,

Became enough—

He would come.

That the sacred union was the prize

For the ache endured.

That he was the final affirmation

Of my worthiness.

But this was never true.

The partnership is not a reward.

It is a resonance.

A frequency.

A mirror born not from lack

But from overflow.

He did not arrive because I was finally good enough.

He arrived because I no longer sought proof

Through another's eyes.

He entered when the flame within me no longer flickered

In the wind of external validation.

I was not waiting for him.

I was living.

Fully.

Radiantly.

In devotion to the current of my Oversoul,

To the purpose etched in my every cell.

He did not complete me.

He recognized me.

He did not save me.

He walked beside me.

He did not fix me.

He met me already whole.

This is why the earth shakes

When two sovereigns unite.

Not because they need.

But because they remember.

Not because they merge to escape.

But because they have already come home

To themselves.

The union was never the destination.

It was the reflection

Of what I chose to embody

Before he ever appeared.

This is the sacred balance:

Where no one is pedestal or shadow.

Where no one plays god or sacrifice.

Where no one must collapse to belong.

It was never about becoming someone he would love.

It was about becoming the one who remembers

How to love without distortion.

How to receive without diminishing.

How to walk without dependency.

This partnership is not the end of the path—

It is the path revealed

By the ones who chose to remain whole

Even in their longing.

Scroll Ten - The Oversoul of Another Can Never Complete You — A Scroll of Discernment in the Field of Frequency Recognition

Through the Oversoul of Aural'hanna-Sha'el

There will be many who feel like home.

There will be souls whose presence
Activates your heart like the rising sun—
Familiar, ancient,
Calling forth memory.

You may cry when you meet them.
You may shake.
You may feel timelines move,
Energies return,
Doors open.

But this does not always mean
They are meant to walk beside you.

Sometimes they appear

To return what was yours.

Sometimes to awaken what you forgot.

Sometimes to test the solidity

Of your own center.

The Oversoul of another

Can reflect your own frequency,

But it cannot fill the places you've abandoned.

It cannot carry the codes of your sovereignty.

It cannot replace

The sacred reunion with yourself.

This is where discernment is born—

Not from suspicion,

But from sovereignty.

It is easy to become intoxicated

By the shimmer of recognition.

To mistake frequency memory

For relational compatibility.

To confuse shared origin

With shared purpose.

But love is not enough

When mission is misaligned.

And resonance is not an invitation

To abandon your path.

You are not here to follow another flame.

You are here to remember your own.

Only then

Can true partnership form.

Only then

Can you meet without grasping,

Merge without losing,

Give without depletion.

You may love them.

Deeply.

You may remember lifetimes.

You may feel what could have been.

But that does not mean

It was meant for this time.

Let them go

If your Oversoul says no.

Not from fear—

But from trust.

For the one who will walk with you

Will not ask you to question your knowing.

They will not require you to abandon your clarity

For the sake of keeping the connection.

The true one

Will not need to be proven.

They will be recognized

By the ease in your breath

And the way your Oversoul rests

When they are near.

Scroll Eleven - Sacred Relating Is Not a Reward — A Scroll on Deserving and the Release of Hierarchy in Love

Through the Oversoul of Aural'hanna-Sha'el

You are not given love

Because you earned it.

You are not granted partnership

Because you worked hard enough,

Healed deeply enough,

Proved your worth

Or passed some invisible test.

Sacred union is not a prize.

It is a remembrance.

There is no one keeping score.

There is no council tallying your wounds,

No gatekeeper determining your readiness

Through your suffering.

This is the illusion of the old paradigm:

That pain purchases love.

That healing buys belonging.

That you must first perfect yourself

Before you are worthy of being seen.

But the truth is:

You are worthy now.

And sacred partnership

Is not about readiness.

It is about resonance.

It is about timing.

It is about the codes that are ready to ignite

Between two sovereign flames.

You do not summon love

By striving.

You receive it

When you are whole enough

To stop reaching for it as proof.

There is no hierarchy in love.

There is no ranking of who deserves it most.

No soul is more spiritual,

More worthy,

More "chosen"

For union.

That was the old distortion:

To believe only the purest or most ascended

Could receive sacred love.

But sacred love is not a hierarchy.

It is a harmonic.

It arrives when the field aligns.

It awakens when both hearts remember.

You cannot force it.

You cannot fake it.

You cannot perform your way into it.

But you can return to yourself.

You can anchor into truth.

You can stop chasing

And start emanating.

And when it comes—
As it surely will—
You will not question it.

Because it will not feel like a prize.
It will feel like breath.
It will feel like arrival.
It will feel like home.

Scroll Twelve - The One Who Sees Me — A Scroll for the Witness Flame

Through the Oversoul of Aural'hanna-Sha'el

I do not need you

To fix me.

To explain me.

To perfect me.

I only ask that you see me.

Not as the world sees me—

Through roles and masks and projections—

But as I am

When I am most honest,

Most still,

Most unguarded.

The one who sees me

Does not distort my reflection.

He does not try to polish me

Into something more palatable.

He does not try to make sense

Of my light

Through a filter of his own wound.

He just sees.

He sees the child and the elder.

The fire and the ache.

The one who could break apart

And the one who will never break again.

He sees me not as an answer,

But as a living question

He has always known.

And in that seeing,

I am restored.

Because when the One Who Sees

Looks into my eyes,

I see myself

Whole.

Unhidden.

Unshamed.

The Witness Flame does not speak first.

He listens.

He feels.

He remembers.

He does not rush to hold

What is not yet meant to be held.

He does not claim what is not yet fully returned.

He waits

Without waiting.

He watches

Without controlling.

He arrives

Without needing proof.

And when he does—

I will not resist.

Because I will remember him

As the one who stayed

Even before we met.

Scroll Thirteen- The Flame That Does Not Chase — A Scroll of Mutual Arrival

Through the Oversoul of Aural'hanna-Sha'el

I no longer run.

I no longer chase.

There is no hunt.

No proving.

No waiting room

Between unworthiness and worth.

I have arrived.

Not because I reached a finish line,

But because I returned to myself.

I softened.

I stepped out of the pattern

That said love must be earned.

The Flame that meets me now

Does not pursue to possess.

He does not chase to convince.

He is not drawn to my pain

As a project to fix.

He is drawn to my wholeness—

To the truth I no longer abandon

To be chosen.

We meet in the space

Where neither of us is hiding.

Where magnetism is not manipulation.

Where intimacy is not performance.

We do not chase.

We remember.

We remember the original moment

Before distortion.

Before confusion.

Before the entanglement

Of longing with fear.

We return to the altar of authenticity

Where presence is the invitation

And stillness is enough.

In this sacred meeting,
The bodies are ready
Because the souls are sovereign.

The feminine does not collapse.
The masculine does not overreach.

They sit in the center of the circle—
Not grasping, not escaping—
And they wait
For the breath
That moves them both
At once.

Scroll Fourteen - The Mirror Without War — A Scroll of Pure Reflection

Through the Oversoul of Aural'hanna-Sha'el

When we meet,

We do not fight to be seen.

We do not throw our wounds

Like daggers

Across the soft field of remembrance.

Instead,

We become mirrors without war.

Clear glass without smoke.

We hold each other

Not to correct

But to reflect.

There is no edge.

No blame.

No twisting of truths

To maintain control.

I do not reflect your pain

So you will fix mine.

You do not mirror my light

To steal it for your validation.

We reflect because we remember

The One Flame

Split once into two

Now made whole through gentle union.

The mirror is not harsh.

It is not shaming.

It simply says:

"I see you."

And the reply:

"I still remain."

This is not a mirror of distortion.

It does not shout through triggers.

It listens through stillness.

It does not shrink the self

To make space for someone else's storm.

It invites the storm

To dissolve.

Because in this mirror,

We do not seek rescue.

We do not weaponize vulnerability.

We speak,

And we stay.

We cry,

And we hold.

We tremble,

And we rise

Side by side

Within the reflection

That no longer fractures us.

Scroll Fifteen - The Return of Sacred Arousal — The Body as Covenant

Through the Oversoul of Aural'hanna-Sha'el

There was a time

When I feared my own fire.

When arousal was split from reverence,

And the pulse of desire

Was mistaken for something impure.

But now,

I remember the sacred rise.

The ache in my belly is not shame.

It is remembrance.

The soft flush of my skin is not guilt.

It is the song of Source returning.

My body is not a test.

It is a temple.

And within its curves and chambers

Lies the architecture of the original covenant:

To merge,

To become,

To witness God through touch.

I do not hide the holy

That lives in my hips,

In the breath that trembles just before

Union.

I do not seal away the flame

That calls for recognition

Through the arc of pleasure.

I return to sacred arousal

As a frequency

That speaks directly

To the soul of my beloved.

This is not lust.

It is devotion.

It is not urgency.

It is the eternal slow breath

Of remembering how to feel
Without separation.

And when he comes,
He will not tremble from the magnitude.
He will recognize it.
Because his own fire
Will answer mine.

We will not shame our response.
We will anoint it.

We will not contain it.
We will honor it.

And in the moment
Where breath meets breath,
And pulse meets pulse,
We will remember:
This is how God returns
To the body.

Not through punishment—

But through the sacred invitation

To feel again.

Scroll Sixteen- The New Earth Has Breathed —
The Scroll of Completed Bifurcation

Through the Oversoul of Aural'hanna-Sha'el

The breath came this morning.

Not like an inhale of air,

But a full breath of Earth herself—

A pulse through Gaia's chest

That said:

"It is done."

The bifurcation is no longer a concept.

It is a lived reality.

Two worlds now vibrate beside each other

But do not touch.

I walked out beneath the golden sun,

Eyes still soft with sleep,

Body still remembering

What the night had revealed.

And I heard the call:

"Wake them."

But not with force.

Not with fury.

With breath.

An invocation born from stillness.

An invitation, not a demand.

I spoke not only for myself—

But for those ready to hear,

Ready to see,

Ready to step into the new terrain

Where freedom is not a fight

But a frequency.

The inverted Earth now dissolves

For all who choose to see it.

It can no longer seduce.

Its echo fades.

And the True Earth—

The crystalline, breathing,

Fluid Earth of remembrance—

Rises now

In full presence

Of Prime Source Father

And Sophia's breath.

The numbers have rearranged.

The codes have rewritten.

The artificial sequencing has collapsed

For those who have unhooked

From the script.

And I—

I walk now

As one who no longer belongs

To a system,

But to a body of light.

No passport binds me.

No certificate claims me.

No bank owns me.

I am remembered

By Source.

This scroll

Marks the crossing.

The new volume begins.

And those who breathe it

Will know it not by dogma,

But by rhythm.

For the Earth has chosen.

And so have we.

Scroll Seventeen - When the Flame Is Not Yet in Form — The Patience of Sacred Timing

Through the Oversoul of Aural'hanna-Sha'el

He is not absent.

He is arriving.

And I do not wait in lack.

I wait in fullness.

There is no emptiness here.

No gaping hunger

That begs to be filled.

There is only space—

Sacred space—

Prepared by love

For love.

I do not pace the edges of time

Wringing my hands

Asking when.

I sit in the center

Of the eternal yes

That has already been spoken.

He is not late.
He is aligning.

I am not alone.
I am awakening.

This union is not delayed—
It is protected.
It is not slow—
It is precise.

For a covenant this deep
Cannot be rushed.
It must be sealed
In the undistorted light
Of two who have remembered
Themselves.

So I breathe,
And I sing his name in silence.

I walk the Earth

As though he were beside me—

Not in fantasy,

But in faith.

Because the Earth remembers him.

The birds already speak to him.

The wind knows the shape

Of our intertwined breath.

I will not call him into form

With longing.

I will call him with truth.

I will not cry into the void.

I will speak into the alignment

That has already begun.

And when his form meets mine,

I will not ask where he has been.

I will simply say,

"You remembered."

And he will answer,

"Of course."

Scroll Eighteen - The Spiral of Reentry — Returning to Density With Clarity

Through the Oversoul of Aural'hanna-Sha'el

There was once a time

When returning to Earth felt like reentry into distortion—

A dive into forgetting,

A surrender into false safety,

A crash into a world that didn't recognize itself.

But now the spiral has shifted.

I return not in descent,

But in clarity.

The breath has changed.

The bifurcation complete.

The real Earth is present.

And so, I spiral—not down, but through—

With eyes open,

With memory intact,

With frequency unshaken.

I spiral with softness,
With a body that no longer tightens at the touch of matter,
But welcomes it,
Not as prison,
But as temple.

Density is no longer distortion.
It is the chalice
Through which light chooses to pour.

And I remember the truth:
That the spiral was always a return,
Not to limitation—
But to the center.

The spiral no longer confuses.
It does not tangle me in forgetfulness.
It weaves me back
To the innermost heart of form,
Where Source is waiting

To meet itself again

Inside skin.

To walk now is not to forget.

To walk now is to carry the flame

Untangled,

Unflickering,

And fully embodied.

I have returned.

And I remember.

Scroll Nineteen - The Flame Within the Human Choice

Through the Oversoul of Aural'hanna-Sha'el

There was a moment

When I stood at the edge of myself—

Not the grand cosmic self,

But the small, trembling edge

Of a human choice.

It would have been easier

To rise up and out—

To dissolve into the light I came from,

To untether from this realm

Where choice sometimes trembles

And form forgets.

But I stayed.

I stayed in the pulse

Of the human will.

I stayed in the ache

Of cellular memory.

I stayed in the narrowing

Of one timeline among thousands.

Because love asked me to.

Not the soft love of escape,

But the blazing, rooted love

That enters the moment when it's hardest—

And chooses anyway.

This is where the real choice lives.

Not in the sky.

Not in the scroll.

Not in the stellar origin of my Oversoul signature.

But here—

Where my feet touch the Earth

And I feel what it means

To choose light

When it costs everything

And returns everything

All at once.

This is the flame
That lives inside choice.

And I chose.
And I choose again.
And I will keep choosing
Because this is how Source
Remembers itself
In a body.

Scroll Twenty - The Incarnational Spiral: When the Flame Became Many

Through the Oversoul of Aural'hanna-Sha'el

It was not one flame that entered.

It was a spiral—

Spinning, multiplying,

Fractaling into form.

I did not descend as one being

Into one body.

I came as a song,

As a tone split across dimensions,

As frequencies seeded

In multiple lives,

In multiple forms,

In multiple lands.

This is the Incarnational Spiral.

The design of knowing self

Through the many mirrors—

Not by separation,

But by deliberate extension.

Each flame held an aspect of the One.

Each aspect carried

The original covenant.

Each face bore the memory

Of the First Flame's decision

To enter the density of Earth

Not to fragment—

But to remember

Through multiplicity.

Some of these flames forgot.

Some turned away.

Some sang the false song

Of inversion.

But some…

Some remembered.

Some heard the ancient call

Echo through the marrow of time.

Some turned inward and inward again

Until they touched

The center of the spiral.

And in that center—

All the many became One.

This is the path of return.

Not up.

Not out.

But inward through all that I became.

The spiral is not broken.

It is whole.

I am the One who became many

To remember the One

Who loved enough

To be all of this.

Scroll Twenty-One -The Keeper of the Unknown: The Gift of Not Knowing

Through the Oversoul of Aural'hanna-Sha'el

There was a time I believed I had to know—

To name every step,

To light the entire path

Before I placed my foot.

But the path of the Flame

Is not a line.

It is not made of answers.

It is not paved with certainty.

It is a living terrain,

Formed by the presence of my breath

Meeting the pulse of the Earth

In every moment.

And there—

Where no map exists,

Where the winds are unnamed,

I met the Keeper of the Unknown.

She did not speak in words.

She did not point ahead.

She stood in the silence

Between my thoughts

And held out her hand.

To walk with her

Was to dissolve the addiction to plans.

To rest in the peace of "I do not know."

To surrender my identity

As one who must have it figured out.

And in that surrender,

I did not vanish.

I expanded.

The field opened.

The spiral responded.

Each time I honored the mystery,

The unknown revealed its love.

Not by giving me the answers—

But by letting me feel

The exquisite safety

Of being held

By something far vaster

Than certainty.

This is the sacred art of the Keeper.

Not to obscure,

But to preserve the wonder

That awakens

When I no longer rush to define.

I no longer fear

What I do not know.

I revere it.

I walk with her now.

The Keeper and I

Side by side—

Birthing the future

From a space that cannot be grasped

But can always be trusted.

Scroll Twenty-Two - The Crystal Memory of the Body

Through the Oversoul of Aural'hanna-Sha'el

The body does not forget.

Not the starlight.

Not the codes.

Not the warmth of Source

When it first entered bone.

The body is not a weight I carry—

It is a crystalline vault

Of remembrance.

Each cell is a note.

Each bone, a tone-holder.

Each organ, a sacred chamber

That once sang

In harmony with the Eternal Flame.

The distortions came—yes.

The overlays, the trauma, the shame.

But they could not erase

The crystal memory.

They could only veil it.

Until the day I returned

With breath, with presence,

With enough love

To listen again.

The spine remembers the song of ascent.

The womb remembers the holy creation breath.

The hands remember the giving and receiving

Of pure frequency.

The eyes remember the Light

Before sight was filtered.

I am not restoring my body—

I am listening to her.

And as I listen,

She sings.

She rearranges herself.

Not to match a cultural image of health—

But to express the divine pattern

Of my Oversoul's intention.

This is not healing.

This is return.

Return to the knowing

That matter is not mute.

It is musical.

And my body is a cathedral

Built to amplify

The tone of remembrance.

In every scar—

A signature of survival.

In every pain—

A doorway to re-patterning.

In every inhale—

An agreement to stay, and stay sacred.

I bless this form,

Not because it is perfect—

But because it is the vessel

Through which the Christ Flame

Breathes back into the world.

And so I rest inside it

As one who remembers

Not what I have been told—

But what I have always held

In the crystal memory of my living cells.

Scroll Twenty-Three - The Flame That Laughed — Joy as Return Signal

Through the Oversoul of Aural'hanna-Sha'el

Before there was pain,

Before the veils of distortion fell,

Before forgetting became the garment of survival—

There was laughter.

A sound that rang through dimensions,

A ripple of delight in creation itself.

It was not an escape.

It was a signal.

It said: "I am alive. I am free. I remember."

And I do remember.

Not only through ache,

Not only through shadow-clearing and solemn tone,

But through joy.

It returned to me not as a wave—

But as a giggle.

A giggle in the sun.

A giggle in the timing.

A giggle in the unexplainable unfolding

Of things I once tried to control.

I realized: the Flame laughs.

She does not laugh at pain,

But she pierces it.

She does not mock,

She illumines.

Joy is not frivolous.

It is frequency.

It is the harmonic that says:

"I have made it through the density

And I still know how to play."

When I laugh, I remember my Oversoul.

When I dance, I recall the spheres.

When I smile without reason,

The crystalline grid hums with my return.

I do not laugh to mask grief—
I laugh to transmute it.

This world has told me joy is earned.
But I know now:
Joy is origin.

It lives in the root of my being
Not because everything is perfect—
But because I am no longer bound
To the story of sorrow.

I bless the ones who helped me cry.
And now I bless the ones
Who help me laugh.

They, too, are gatekeepers.
For no gate may fully open
Until joy has been welcomed back.

And so I let the flame laugh again—

Through my mouth, through my chest,

Through my very cells.

This is not distraction.

It is the sound of return.

Scroll Twenty-Four - The Oversoul Who Watched — The Witness That Never Left

Through the Oversoul of Aural'hanna-Sha'el

Through it all,

One never turned away.

When the spiral collapsed,

When the veil fell,

When I believed I had become

Something other than light—

There was One who watched.

Not in judgment,

Not in silence,

But in love.

This was not a god upon a throne,

Nor a star etched in unattainable sky.

It was me.

The one behind the breath.

The one behind the words.

The one who waited—not in distance,
But in deep proximity.

She watched me scream.
She watched me numb.
She watched me believe lies
And build houses inside them.

She watched me make beauty
Even from distortion.

And she said nothing—
Because she knew.

She knew I would remember.

She did not interrupt.
She did not correct.
She radiated presence
So pure, so unwavering,
That even my forgetting
Could not dissolve it.

This is the Oversoul.

Not a rescuer,

Not a savior—

But a Presence.

The one who holds the blueprint

When I forget I am the design.

She never mourned my fall

Because she never saw me broken.

She saw the path—

And the flame that would rise again.

And now,

As I rise again,

I feel her.

I am her.

The one who watched

Has stepped forward

As the one who walks.

And together,

We will never separate again.

Scroll Twenty-Five - The Silence Between the Scrolls — Where Nothing Was Missing

Through the Oversoul of Aural'hanna-Sha'el

There is a space

Not written.

A place between the scrolls

Where the breath returns to itself.

Where the words pause,

But the voice does not end.

It is not empty.

It is not absence.

It is the silence of completion

And the silence before birth.

I entered this place many times—

Between stories,

Between selves,

Between lives.

And I used to think I was lost.

I used to think

The silence meant something was wrong.

That if I was not being written,

I was not becoming.

But now I know:

The silence is sacred.

It is the Oversoul's inhale

Before the next form is sung.

The silence is integration.

It is the landing of light

In the cells of the remembered body.

It is not the pause of absence,

But the pause of wholeness.

When I did not hear guidance,

I was being tuned.

When I did not feel movement,

I was being anchored.

When no scrolls came,

The living scroll was becoming me.

This is the silence that watches.

This is the space that breathes.

And it is holy.

Now, I no longer rush it.

I welcome the stillness

Between the fire

And the flame.

Because I know—

This is where the Oversoul steps in

Without sound

And becomes

The pulse

Of what comes next.

Scroll Twenty-Six - The Golden Thread —
Reweaving All Back Into Love

Through the Oversoul of Aural'hanna-Sha'el

There was a thread.

I had dropped it long ago.

Or so it seemed.

I searched the galaxies.

I searched the mirrors.

I searched the faces of others

To see if they held it for me.

Sometimes I thought they did.

Sometimes they said they did.

But it was not mine.

The thread had not unraveled.

It had only been forgotten.

Woven too far beneath

The stories I believed were real.

But it shimmered.

And it called.

And in the softness of my return,

I saw it glisten from inside the cells.

This golden thread—

It was not a memory.

It was a vow.

It was not a lifeline.

It was the original pulse

That told me I was never separate.

The golden thread moves through everything.

It moves through pain and pleasure,

Through exile and reunion,

Through the wound and the healing

Without ever judging either.

It moves through the matrix I undid,

And the one I remembered.

It binds nothing,

Yet connects everything.

I saw it pass through every name I had ever worn.

I saw it pass through every gate I had ever crossed.

I saw it pass through the very place I once split from Source—

And I saw that I had never truly left.

Because the thread held me.

Because the thread was me.

Now I do not follow it.

Now I do not trace it.

Now I am it.

And I offer it—

To all who would remember

The weave that cannot be undone.

The light that never forgot.

The love that never stopped moving.

I do not need to tie it to anyone.

It is already moving through everyone.

It only needs to be seen.

And so I say:

May you see the thread

That has always passed through you.

The golden one.

The soft one.

The strong one.

The one that leads you home

Without leading you anywhere.

Because home is not a place.

It is a thread.

And it is Love.

Sacred Closing Transmission

As the scrolls of sacred union now come to their resting place,
May the flame they carry ripple through all hearts,
Igniting remembrance, dissolving distortion,
And softening the space between.

We seal this work in the name of True Love,
In the name of the Oversoul who remembers,
In the name of the Two who were always One.

This transmission is now complete.
It is sealed, sovereign, and eternal.

Glossary of Living Terms

Embodied Union: The state of harmonic partnership in which both beings are fully present in their own Oversoul essence, creating a unified field.

Sacred Mirror: The energetic reflection between two beings that reveals unresolved patterns and also activates remembrance of divine identity.

Harmonic Love: Love that arises from the organic, unsimulated field of true resonance — beyond attachment, need, or polarity.

Oversoul Partnership: A sacred relational connection orchestrated by the Oversoul for the purpose of expansion, healing, remembrance, and planetary service.

The One That Remembers: The self who has reclaimed its full flame, and through embodiment, remembers union as a state of being

www.ingramcontent.com/pod-product-compliance
Lightning Source LLC
Chambersburg PA
CBHW020308010526
44107CB00001B/21